FRAMEWORK PROFESSIONAL DEVELOPMENT:

Self-study Modules for Teachers and Lecturers

DEVELOP BETTER TEACHER-PUPIL RELATIONSHIPS IN YOUR CLASSROOM

Roger Smith

Framework Press Educational Publishers Ltd.
Parkfield
Greaves Road
LANCASTER
LA1 4TZ

First published 1996

ISBN 1 85008 133 6

FRAMEWORK PROFESSIONAL DEVELOPMENT:
Self-study Modules for Teachers and Lecturers
DEVELOP BETTER TEACHER-PUPIL RELATIONSHIPS
IN YOUR CLASSROOM

A catallogue record for the book is available from the British Library

Typeset by AMA Graphics Ltd., Preston

Printed in Great Britain
by The Charlesworth Group, Huddersfield

Cover design by John Angus
Illustrations by Trevor Green

Table of Contents

The Author:

Roger Smith has worked in schools, a college of Further Education, the Open University and the University of Warwick. He has taught INSET courses, published widely and broadcast on BBC Radio. Seven photocopiable packs have been published by Framework Press: *The Effective School, Volume 1: Teachers Working Together: The Whole School Approach* (1990); *The Effective School, Volume 2: Classroom Techniques and Management* (1990); *The Heads' and Deputies' Handbook: Managing Schools in the 1990s* (1992); *Managing Pupil Behaviour in School and Classroom: In-house Training Materials for Teachers* (1993); *Preparing for Appraisal: Self-evaluation for Teachers in Primary and Secondary Schools* (1993); *Preparing for Inspection: The Whole School Approach* (1994) and *Managing Your Classroom: A Guide to Better Teaching* (1994). In this series of handbooks, he has produced *Develop Your Classroom Management Skills* (1995) and *Preparing Yourself for Inspection* (1995). As the Headteacher of a large Combined School, he has been involved in many committees and planning groups. He also works in the Education Department of the University of Warwick.

Editor:

Karen Westall

Acknowledgements:

The author would like to thank the many people who have contributed directly and indirectly to the thinking that has culminated in this book, especially all those colleagues, tutors, teachers, course and conference members who have helped, often without knowing, to shape the ideas expressed here. He also wishes to thank particularly his wife, children and friends for their support.

Introduction

It seems reasonable to assume that the better and the more positive the relationships between teachers and pupils, the easier it will be to teach and learn effectively. Most successful teachers establish classroom relationships which enable pupils to relate to and work alongside each other and, whilst the focus of this handbook is on teacher-pupil relationships, there is an assumption that if these work well, pupils' relationships with each other will benefit.

Teachers are able to improve relationships because they develop a classroom ethos which is based on a sense of FIRMNESS, FAIRNESS and CONSISTENCY. Without this framework of good classroom management, caring and supportive discipline and a mutual and positive respect between teachers and pupils, very little in the way of high quality teaching and learning will develop. What this handbook will do is suggest various strategies, which, if used consistently, will help you establish the kinds of relationships in your classroom which will maximise your chances of teaching well.

One of the first areas this handbook explores is the kind of teacher you are. It asks you to look at yourself as a teacher and consider what has influenced the way you work with pupils in your classroom.

In later Units, you will examine successful classroom atmospheres and the kinds of rules and sanctions that operate within your particular style of classroom management. In these Units, there is an assumption that you will need to be an assertive teacher, who is able to respond to individuals as well as to the class as a whole and who can obtain good classroom control and maintain high quality relationships without either being openly aggressive to the pupils you teach or so passive that they, rather than you, control events.

When you are working through the Units, it is important that you think about your own teaching in your school. After all, the book has been written to help you improve your teaching skills, but it is also important to reflect on your own practice so that you learn from any mistakes and build on your many successes.

UNIT 1
What Makes You the Teacher You Are?

It is very important to reflect on what you do well and what you do less well in your classroom.

It is equally true that you must be aware of what you find easy and what you find difficult to do, especially when pupils misbehave or are disruptive.

When you are examining techniques of control, discipline and classroom management and are working out strategies to improve teacher-pupil relationships, you are bound to be more satisfied with some of your skills than you are with others. Your personality may influence what you are able to do well. What colleagues can do easily, and the techniques they use, may well be very difficult for you to develop as part of your teaching strategy. Effective teachers are usually good at recognising the positive benefits of reflecting on their successes in every aspect of school life.

It is certainly important to recognise what is successful when you are establishing a working pupil-teacher relationship.

◆ ACTIVITY 1.1 ◆◆◆

Here are six real descriptions of memories of school life. Some apply to experiences in infant schools and some to secondary. It doesn't matter because they are real experiences applicable across the age ranges.

Read each one and use the spaces to write your responses.

1. 'I remember once when I was about five or six and I couldn't write. I was told to come out to the front of the class and write "a" on the blackboard and, when I couldn't do it, the teacher kept making me try over and over again in front of everybody.'
What kind of atmosphere might this kind of teaching create?

Imagine what you would do in this situation. How should the teacher handle it? What kind of teacher-pupil relationship should the teacher be trying to create?

What is better about the relationships that you are trying to create?

2. 'What I remember is really simple and a bit silly. It was when I started secondary school. I hadn't got the right kind of coloured pencils to shade this map in; I don't think I even knew I was supposed to have them. Anyway this teacher shouted at me really loudly for ages in front of all my new friends.'

What kind of pupil-teacher relationship would develop from this kind of scenario?

What would you have done?

What kind of relationship with the pupil and the class would you have tried to create?

3. 'My happiest times were in the sixth form, when at last teachers started using my first name and talking to me as if I was a human being. They seemed to see you as someone that mattered.'

What could you do in your classroom that would make these kinds of positive relationships develop lower down the school?

How do you show your pupils that they are individuals who matter?

4. 'I went on a brilliant school trip to France. All the teachers suddenly became human beings and laughed and smiled and were really friendly.'

How do you make sure that the relationships you establish are friendly?

As a teacher, do you think your pupils see you as a human being? How do you know?

5. 'We had this really scruffy male teacher. His belly used to hang over his trousers and you could see it through the gap in his shirt. He had dirty fingernails and his breath always smelled of tobacco when he leaned over you to mark anything. One Monday, my friend and I had both had our hair cut really short and spiky. When he had us in his class he just went on about how stupid it looked over and over again.'

What sort of behaviour should the teacher in this extract be modelling?

What do you do if it is obvious pupils have changed their appearance in some way?

6. 'I was terrible at PE and Games and we had one of those stereotypical PE teachers. He always praised the boys and thought girls were rubbish. He used to pick on me when I was about thirteen to demonstrate things I was really bad at. I hated it and sometimes used to cry.'

What is the teacher doing wrong?

What would you do that would prevent this kind of breakdown in relationships?

♦ ACTIVITY 1.2 ◆◆◆

All the quotes in *Activity 1.1* were real. They were made by undergraduates training to be teachers when they were asked to describe, in very broad terms, some highlights and low spots of their relationships with teachers during their time at school. It is a sad reflection on the English education system that they all, and this involved over 100 students, found it easier to think of bad experiences than good ones.

Look back at your responses to the questions in *Activity 1.1*. They will have raised some broad issues relating to how to create positive relationships and how negative ones might develop. So let's make a start and identify the kinds of teacher behaviour we would like to use as well as the kind of teacher behaviour we would like to discourage.

Using your responses in *Activity 1.1*, fill in the following chart:

Teacher Behaviour which will Affect Teacher-Pupil Relationships

Teacher behaviour *I wish to develop*	*Teacher behaviour* *I wish to stop*

◆ ACTIVITY 1.3 ◆◆◆

In *Activity 1.2*, you were asked to suggest those broad areas of teacher behaviour which would encourage good, successful and effective teacher-pupil relationships. Let's stick to the positive for the time being and leave the negative behaviour which would discourage good relationships.

There must be certain teaching skills which, if used well, should make it easier to develop positive relationships. Whatever kind of teacher you are, it would be useful to think about some of these skills and how you would use them.

Here are twelve effective skills. Read each one and first of all tick the appropriate box. Please be honest and truthful, because you are being asked whether it applies to you *Not often, Often* or *Very often*. In other words do you, as a teacher, use this skill or not?

Before moving on to the next statement, use the space below each one to write down how using this skill could develop positive and successful pupil-teacher relationships and how it would lead to good practice.

I am involved in out-of-school activities.

Twelve Effective Skills

I am good at developing positive pupil-teacher relationships because I am . . .	*Not often*	*Often*	*Very often*
1. . . . punctual and reliable			
2. . . . committed to further training			
3. . . . a good team member			
4. . . . able to plan and set objectives both in the long and short term			
5. . . . involved in out-of-school activities			

6. . . . able to maintain good relations with pupils and command respect			
7. . . . capable of using a variety of teaching styles			
8. . . . able to explain plans and objectives to pupils clearly			
9. . . . able to communicate with parents, governors and the school's community			
10. . . . aware of the resources that are available and appropriate for different purposes			

11. . . . capable of developing a thorough and helpful marking schedule			
12. . . . able to teach and assess at the same time			

◆ ░ **ACTIVITY 1.4** ░ ◆◆◆

If you are not particularly good at a specific teaching skill, it follows that you should either stop using it or learn how to use it more effectively. At the same time, if you are good at something, you need to keep doing it as successfully as possible.

Think about these questions and use the space to write some brief notes.

How are you going to learn to use those skills that you aren't particularly good at? Who will help you learn how to use them?

How are you going to make sure that you keep using those skills that you are good at? If it is possible for you to help someone else use the skills you are good at, how would you go about it?

◆ ACTIVITY 1.5 ◆◆◆

Here is a case study. It could have happened in your classroom and in your school. It is about classroom management, skills of control and the strategies required to respond to challenging behaviour. It is also about what *you*, as a teacher, would do in this situation.

Read it and respond to the questions in the space below. You may wish to discuss your responses with a trusted colleague.

Case study

It is the first day back after the October half-term. One girl in your tutor group has returned to school as disruptive as she was during the first half-term. Your relationship with her was very poor and you can see no way that it will improve. She shouts out answers, talks loudly to her friends across the room, yells if anyone looks at her or tries to borrow anything and blames her partner if she makes mistakes in her book. She often can't do the work and says it is too easy or boring.

Her sister, in another class, is causing similar problems and several parents have rung the school to complain of bullying, both in school and outside during weekends. It is Tuesday and, after a loud altercation with her, she has run out of the classroom saying that she is going home. In your desk is a letter from her mother pleading for help for both her and her sister. It is the school's policy to respond to such letters within three working days.

First of all, what skills would you use to control her challenging behaviour?

At the same time as you are controlling the behaviour, how would you establish better teacher-pupil relationships?

What kind of response to the parent's letter would be the most helpful?

◆ ACTIVITY 1.6 ◆◆◆

In this Activity, you will need to look honestly at your teaching style(s).

Read each of the following teacher behaviours. In the space alongside each one write:

> O . . . If you behave in this way often
> U . . . If you behave in this way usually
> N . . . If you never behave in this way

1. Do you arrive before the class is due to start?	
2. Do you arrive well prepared?	
3. Do you expect to give and receive respect?	
4. Do you treat everyone as an individual?	
5. Do you smile and say hello to your pupils?	
6. Do you accept the occasional pupil problem as an inevitable part of growing up?	
7. Do you listen when pupils are talking to you?	
8. Do you use punishment sparingly?	
9. Do you set high standards?	
10. Do you apply rules fairly and consistently?	
11. Do you deal with all misbehaviour?	
12. Do you extend and motivate all pupils?	
13. Do you enjoy yourself?	
14. Do you use pupils' first names?	
15. Do you put examples of all your pupils' work on display at some time during the year?	
16. Do you avoid confrontation?	
17. Do you avoid humiliating pupils?	
18. Do you avoid over-reacting?	

19. Do you avoid blanket punishments, i.e. punishing the whole class for the bad behaviour of one person?	
20. Do you avoid punishing more often than you praise?	
21. Do you avoid sarcasm?	

◆ ACTIVITY 1.7 ◆◆◆

Some teacher behaviour on the lists in *Activity 1.6* will be more useful than others in establishing good teacher-pupil relationships. If you are working through this material with colleagues, it would be helpful to try and reach consensus about what kind of teacher behaviour is the most successful.

What I would like to make clear is that if you have answered *never* to any of the first 15 questions perhaps you need to ask yourself whether what you do is as helpful as it could be.

Rather than go through each aspect of teacher behaviour in *Activity 1.6*, let's ask a simple question: What would happen if . . .?

If you are working with colleagues, each one of the questions below could be used as a starting point for discussion. If you are working on your own, think carefully about each one and how your decision might increase your own efforts to improve relationships in your classroom? There are spaces to respond briefly.

What would happen if you didn't listen when pupils were talking to you?

What would happen if you didn't try to extend and motivate all pupils?

What would happen if you didn't see the occasional behaviour problem as part of growing up but saw each one as a personal insult?

What would happen to the ethos of your class if you constantly used humiliation as a basic control technique?

What would happen if your pupils knew that you hated teaching them and were miserable all the time?

What would happen if blanket punishments were used frequently?

What would happen to the ethos of your classroom if punishments were used more frequently than praise?

❖

What would happen if you didn't listen when pupils were talking to you?

◆ ACTIVITY 1.8 ◆◆◆

This Activity contains two definitions. The first one is of a colleague who is not a particularly good teacher and who does not build up very helpful teacher-pupil relations. The other definition is of a colleague who has a good relationship with his/her pupils.

> A less effective colleague is unsure about how to control deviant behaviour and probably creates a narrow, teacher-guided environment, where little tolerance for the individual is encouraged and punishment rather than praise is the norm. There is ample opportunity for on-task working, but there are frequent bouts of off-task behaviour. Expectations may well be lower, and the outcomes of a predictable sameness.

> An effective colleague has few discipline problems and gives pupils the opportunity to grow and develop in a variety of ways with a variety of outcomes, in an atmosphere of tolerance, high expectations and on-task working.

Write down *four* of your teaching characteristics that are *Effective*, and four that are *Less effective*. Be totally honest. It is the only way to learn about the kind of teacher you are and what you need to change.

	Effective	*Less effective*
1.		
2.		
3.		
4.		

Establishing the Right Relationships

♦ **ACTIVITY 2.1** ♦♦♦

If we are trying to establish good relationships, where every pupil is able to learn, we have to be able to do two things in the classroom.

First of all, we must behave in a way that creates an atmosphere where the pupil-teacher relationships are good. Secondly, we must avoid creating situations where pupils can behave badly and where they are able to see that relationships are poor.

✤ *A provocative teacher* will, because of the way s/he behaves, provoke difficult relationships.

✤ *An insulating teacher* will behave in such a way that pupils and teachers are able to work well together.

Read each list of characteristics.

A provocative teacher:

— assumes that pupils don't want to work and, when they don't work, assumes that it is impossible to provide the right conditions;

— believes that discipline is a confrontation that has to be won;

— is unable to defuse situations;

— frequently issues unreal ultimatums which lead to more confrontations;

— uses inconsistent punishments;

— gives preferential treatment to pupils who conform;

— always expects deviant pupils to behave badly;

— makes negative comments about pupils in public;

— avoids contact with pupils outside the classroom.

An insulating teacher:

— assumes that everyone wants to work, and if they don't, the conditions, rather than the pupils, are at fault;

— avoids any kind of favouritism;

— avoids confrontation;

— hardly ever makes any kind of negative comment about pupils in public;

— gives pupils the opportunity to back down and save face when they have to be punished;

— assumes that pupils will behave well;

— cares about and trusts pupils;

— enjoys pupils' company both inside and outside the classroom.

If you have a colleague who is using this material, discuss the following questions with him/her and then respond in the spaces.

If you are on your own, think about your answers and write your responses in the spaces.

Will all pupils respond to INSULATING skills? Give reasons for your answer.

Are there ever times when you could build up good relationships by being PROVOCATIVE? Give reasons.

Does your classroom teaching style and method of managing your classroom make it possible to use INSULATING skills rather than being PROVOCATIVE? Give your reasons.

What are the most difficult INSULATING skills to use? Why?

What are the most difficult PROVOCATIVE statements to avoid using? Why?

◆ ACTIVITY 2.2 ◆◆◆

Being an insulating teacher is not just about being able to use the skills suggested in *Activity 2.1* and avoid being provocative.

Here are three further statements about encouraging good relationships. Each one is followed by a short case study and some questions. There are spaces for your responses.

1. What happens in your classroom and the kinds of relationships that are established will depend to a large extent on the successful links between home and school. Good relationships often improve if there are close links between teachers and parents and when the values of both are similar. This is very important and well worth considering as part of your strategy for developing worthwhile pupil-teacher relationships.

Case study 1

John is from a large family and his father has been in prison. Several of his brothers are known to the police. Like many of the family, John is becoming more and more aggressive and produces little or no work. Other pupils are very frightened of him. He has been caught hitting a smaller boy and his reply is: 'So what? My dad says I can hit who I like.'

How might you begin to reduce John's aggression?
What would you say to John about his attitude to his work? How would you begin to change his attitude?
You have arranged to see John's father. How would you run the interview? What points would you want to get across?

2. In any relationship with a pupil, the teacher needs to be able to listen to what the pupil has to say, both inside and outside the classroom.

Case study 2

One of your tutor group has been caught by another teacher with his hand in another pupil's lunch box. It was during registration time. The pupil is spluttering with indignation and saying such things as:

'You are always picking on me.'

'Why are you always fingering me for stealing?'

'Everybody else does it. Why don't you pick on them?'

Your colleague is equally indignant and blames him totally for a series of thefts from bags outside his classroom.

What could the consequences of not listening to the pupil be?
How would you go about listening to him? Where would you do it?
Your colleague has brought him to you. What kind of relationship between you and your colleague would help you to solve this problem?

◆ ACTIVITY 2.3 ◆◆◆

The Activities so far should have suggested to you the importance of establishing positive relationships with the pupils you teach.

The Elton Report (1989), takes the idea of relationships a step further by relating it to concepts such as: 'popularity' and 'classroom climate'. Teachers who can achieve these good relationships are described in the following ways:

'(They) create a classroom climate in which pupils lose rather than gain popularity with their classmates by causing trouble. They can also spot a disruptive incident in the making, choose an appropriate tactic to deal with it and nip it in the bud. In their relationships with their pupils they always seem to know what is going on behind their backs. Good group managers understand how groups of young people react to each other and to teachers. They also understand and are in full control of their own behaviour. They model the good behaviour they expect from pupils. *All this requires an impressive range of skills.*' (my italics) (pp. 67–68, para.6)

Building up and sustaining relationships is difficult but it must be part of your repertoire of skills, strategies and styles.

The following list both complements and extends the skills statements in *Unit 1*.

Read each statement carefully and, honestly, tick the appropriate box, depending on whether it applies to you *Not often, Often* or *Very often*. Then, before moving on to the next statement, use the space below each one to suggest very briefly why having this particular skill will help you to be better at building up pupil-teacher relationships in your classroom.

An effective teacher is 'all seeing'.

More Effective Skills

An effective teacher . . .	Not often	Often	Very often
1. . . . knows his/her pupils' names, friends and personalities			
2. . . . is flexible and able to take advantage of unexpected events, e.g. pupil's new baby sibling, return from an exotic holiday, a newly broken arm			

3. . . . is continually aware of what is happening by moving around and being 'all seeing'			
4. . . . plans and organises in order to maximise learning opportunities			
5. . . . arranges the layout of the classroom in terms of furniture and space in order to maximise learning opportunities			
6. . . . matches work to pupils' abilities			

7. . . . paces lessons so that there are no negatively pressurised rushes and no periods of inaction			
8. . . . models the kind of polite and acceptable behaviour that will encourage good relationships			
9. . . . improves relationships by being sparing in the use of reprimands			
10. . . . always criticises the behaviour rather than the person			

11. . . . avoids using group punishments by being capable of finding the right culprit			
12. . . . is fair and consistent and builds up relationships by reprimanding pupils privately rather than publicly			

◆ ACTIVITY 2.4 ◆◆◆

After completing *Activity 2.3*, it is important to think about your responses. If you are doing some of this work with colleagues, it will be useful to discuss it with them. One way of focusing your attention is to choose the three or four most important statements from *Activity 2.3*. Choosing them might be difficult. Bear in mind the following points:

✤ Do I use this skill often?

✤ Does it work most of the time?

✤ Would it be useful for everyone?

✤ Is it an essential skill to have?

✤ Could I teach without it?

When you have identified three or four key skills, respond to this final question.

> How have these important skills helped to create or maintain better relationships? Give examples.

◆ **ACTIVITY 2.5** ◆◆◆

If you look back at *Case study 1* on p. 22, it becomes obvious that parents have an important role to play in promoting good relationships, better work ethics, better behaviour and more appropriate attitudes in their children, of whatever age. Most parents will try to be as supportive as possible towards the school. Such parents need nurturing but schools must also find ways of encouraging the support of those parents who feel less able to develop positive links. This latter group of parents, for example, might be less likely to visit school and might find it more difficult to support and develop the attitudes their children need in order to be successful.

Let's look at the links between home and school which might help improve home-school and teacher-pupil relationships.

Read each of the following statements carefully and respond to each one in the spaces.

If you are not doing what the statement suggests, write down why not.

Relationships with Parents

How do you create a welcoming atmosphere for parents who come into school?

How are parents involved in the classroom? (This is probably only applicable in infant and junior schools.)

How are parents involved at home with school work?

How can you use parents and involve them in careers education and work experience?

How do you maintain good channels of written communication?

How do you make parents' evenings and open evenings welcoming and worthwhile?

How do you make sure that the parents of pupils in your class are aware of the school rules, behaviour policies, etc.?

◆ **ACTIVITY 2.6** ◆◆◆

This Activity involves several *Case studies*. They are all fictitious, but they could be going to happen in your school tomorrow.

They are all about relationships in the school and in the classroom.

Read each one and respond to the questions in the spaces. You may wish to compare your responses with those of a trusted colleague.

Case study 1

You have a girl in your class whose behaviour is deteriorating. Your head of department has no sympathy with you or her and suggests that what she needs is 'plenty of book work and a good shouting at'. If this doesn't work, she must stay in at breaks and during lunchtime. The head of department says that she will send a letter home telling the girl's parents what is happening and telling them to come into school to discuss her behaviour. It is rumoured that the girl's mother can be violent and abusive.

Do you think that the suggestions made in the case study will work in preventing bad behaviour and building up a positive teacher-pupil relationship?
What techniques might you try in the classroom?
How would you involve the girl's parents?
What other agencies might you involve?

Case study 2

A girl in your class has told her parents that you are always picking on her. She has been in trouble out of school in the evening with some other pupils in your class. Their parents are blaming this one particular girl, saying that she is the ring leader who is leading their daughters astray. She has certainly been challenging in the classroom and you have had to impose sanctions quite regularly. On this particular day she is saying that no one likes her and accusing you of hating her.

What would your first action be?
What kinds of things would you say to her?

How would you deal with each group of parents?

◆ **ACTIVITY 2.7** ◆◆◆

As a final short Activity, you will need to complete a mini-action plan.

Before you do this, it is important to remember that the more successful the school, the better the teacher-pupil relationships are and the more time and effort is put into making sure that they remain effective.

Write down your responses to the following two statements.

I want to improve the following relationships in my classroom.

I want to use the following classroom management and teaching skills to improve teacher-pupil relationships.

UNIT

3

What is the Most Successful
Classroom Atmosphere?

◆ **ACTIVITY 3.1** ◆◆◆

I want to start this Unit with some very broad ideas about creating a classroom atmosphere where there are excellent opportunities for teaching and learning.

There are five basic principles which, if used consistently, should help you create a positive atmosphere and better teacher-pupil and pupil-pupil relationships in your classroom.

Read each one and then respond in the spaces.

1. *Let your pupils know that you value them*

All of us need to see ourselves as worthwhile and able to succeed. Pupils need to be treated with respect, valued as individuals and encouraged to work to their potential.

What do you do to let your pupils know that you value them?
What might happen if your pupils feel undervalued?

2. *Teach lessons that are relevant to your pupils*

The National Curriculum, tests and exams will dictate much of what you will have to teach. But you, as the teacher, will interpret this content into interesting and relevant experiences for your pupils. It is important to know your pupils, their interests, their strengths and their weaknesses. By observing, listening and discussing with them, you will know what activities are likely to stimulate them, how you will teach and how you will help them to learn and move their learning forward.

Make a short list of how you will begin to plan in this way in your classroom.

What is likely to happen to relationships if you don't plan a curriculum that is relevant to your pupils?

3. *Help your pupils to achieve success*

Unless pupils achieve some success in an activity, or at least see some progress, they will not continue to work well in the classroom. If they do experience success, they are more likely to want to repeat the activity, or one that is similar. Within any class, there may be a wide range of ability and achievement. It will be important to differentiate and provide work that is suitable for all abilities. At the same time, it is equally important to challenge all your pupils so that they maintain interest and experience success by knowing that they have achieved something that was not too easy.

How do you help your pupils to achieve success?

What will happen to the relationships in the classroom if you don't teach in a way that ensures your pupils will achieve some success?

4. *Set appropriate objectives*

When you plan your lessons and know what activities will take place in your classroom, you also need to be able to set objectives. These are what you actually expect each pupil to achieve. If you are not clear about what is to be achieved from a particular activity, neither will the pupils have a sense of its purpose. If they don't have your sense of purpose, they may set their own. These may not necessarily be educational ones.

How do you set objectives in your lessons? What do you need to know about your pupils?

What specific problems will occur if you don't set appropriate objectives for your pupils?

5. *Plan the organisation of your classroom*

The way in which you lay out the furniture in your classroom and how you organise pupil groupings is an important part of your classroom management strategy. Whole class teaching, friendship groups, ability groups, single sex groups, etc. will all determine how you teach and how your pupils learn and relate to you and to each other. In fact these organising structures need to be used flexibly so that your pupils have varied experiences.

How do you arrange your classroom? Why do you do it in this way and what do you hope to achieve?

What problems occur when you arrange your classroom in certain ways?

◆ ACTIVITY 3.2 ◆◆◆

If you develop strategies based on the five issues raised in *Activity 3.1*, you should be able to achieve positive relationships. You need to remember to be *consistent* and to use the strategies repeatedly. At the same time, you need to be seen by all pupils to be *fair* and *firm* in all your dealings with them. You will certainly not be able to build up a successful classroom atmosphere without establishing CODES OF CONDUCT. At the same time as setting up these behaviour parameters, you will also have to let your pupils know the kinds of SANCTIONS you intend to use.

List some of the important RULES or CODES OF CONDUCT that you expect in your classroom and alongside each one write the kind of SANCTION you might use if the rule is broken.

The same sanction could be used for different kinds of rule breaking.

Rule/code of conduct	Sanction

◆ ACTIVITY 3.3 ◆◆◆

In this Activity, examples of sanctions lettered A, B, C, etc. are given. There is then a second list of rules or codes of conduct numbered 1, 2, 3, etc.

Read each *Code of conduct* and write after it the letter or letters, (there may be more than one), of the *Sanctions* you would use if the rule or code was disobeyed. There are spaces for you to add further sanctions and codes of conduct.

As you decide on the appropriate sanction(s), write P if you feel that the sanction will promote positive relationships or N if you feel that this will have a negative or detrimental effect on the relationships in your classroom.

Sanctions

A   Reprimand by teacher

B   Reprimand plus referral to another teacher, e.g. head of year

C   Sent out of the classroom

D   Moved away from friends

E   Withdrawal of breaks

F   Withdrawal of games, PE, etc.

G   A report system where the pupil has to report to you every hour for you to check his/her work/behaviour or a similar system where the pupil reports to another colleague.

H   Letter home complaining of behaviour, attitude, work rate, etc.

I   Detention after school

Other sanctions you would like to add:

J

K

L

M

N

O

P

Codes of Conduct

	Sanction(s)	P/N
1. Always speak politely to everyone: teachers, adults, each other.		
2. Move around the classroom without running or shouting.		
3. Always have the correct equipment with you for the lesson.		
4. Enter and leave the classroom quietly and calmly.		
5. No chewing or eating.		
6. Verbal and physical violence is not allowed.		
7. Teasing other pupils is not allowed.		
8. Do not interfere with anyone else's property.		
9.		
10.		
11.		
12.		

❖

Always have the correct equipment for lessons.

◆ ACTIVITY 3.4 ◆◆◆

If possible, it would be very useful to discuss *Activity 3.3* with colleagues. In this way, you would be able to share wider views on rules and sanctions.

This Activity can be completed on your own, or with a colleague after discussion.

Which are the most common sanctions used?
Why do they work?
Are there certain rules which are more difficult to enforce than others?
Is it important to impose the chosen sanctions fairly or is it possible to pick and choose where and when you use them?

◆ ACTIVITY 3.5 ◆◆◆

Here are some more case studies. They describe various incidents that happen in many schools, maybe even yours. Some of the incidents happen in classrooms and others involve pupils you teach but occur in and around the school. Both types of incident can impinge on the relationships you are trying to develop and need solving in such a way as to promote the best kind of classroom relationships. Beneath each case study there are spaces for your responses. Remember, when you are dealing with each problem, you are trying to develop and sustain the best possible classroom atmosphere where positive relationships can flourish.

If you can, it would be helpful to discuss your responses with a colleague. In this way, you would share ideas.

There are some different approaches suggested in *Case study 1*. Use them as suggestions to help you look at the pros and cons of varying approaches.

Case study 1

A boy runs out of the classroom (and sometimes out of school) whenever there are problems with you, other teachers or other pupils. Usually, he has gone straight home and you have been able to telephone his parents immediately. Recently, he has stopped doing this and has been seen wandering around the town centre shops.

How would you begin to deal with this problem? e.g. Initiate discussions with the boy, try to find the kinds of incidents which trigger the running away, ask for counselling . . .
Are there any classroom sanctions that might stop him doing this? e.g. Keep him in to complete missed work, stand by the door, give him extra work when he does it again . . .

Case study 2

A group of pupils from your class or tutor group have been extremely rude to the cleaners after a football match. On one particular day they spat at one of the women cleaners and now, on the next morning, they are laughing about it.

What would your first move be?

What sanctions would you use?

What would you do if it happened again?

Case study 3

Several pupils in your class have had their packed lunches tampered with. Whoever did it has taken drinks, partly eaten the sandwiches and stolen any chocolate bars. Several other pupils have quietly told you who they think it is. They think that the culprit is a loud, aggressive girl in your class whose parents are going through a difficult divorce.

How do you deal with this problem so that peace, calm and appropriate relationships prosper in the classroom?
How can you make sure that it doesn't happen again?
What kind of discussion will you want to have with the girl whom other pupils are blaming?

Case study 4

One of your pupil's trainers has been stuffed down a toilet and urinated on. A letter from his mother expresses severe displeasure and is demanding that something should be done about the incident.

What will you do first?
What will you say to the victim?
How will you explain to your class or tutor group how you feel about the incident?
What will you say to the parents which will boost their confidence in you and maintain good relationships?

Case study 5

One of the boys in your class has been stealing money from home, buying sweets with it and then sharing them with others in the class. Everyone takes the sweets, but no one wants to be his friend.

What does this kind of incident say about the relationships that exist between these pupils?
What can you do to improve these relationships and prevent this kind of behaviour happening again?

Case study 6

Two of your pupils come running into your classroom. As they sprint through the door, they knock down another pupil who becomes distressed. They seem to find it quite amusing.

What will you say to the pupil who is distressed?

What will you say to the two pupils who have run through the door?

What will you do to prevent this happening again?

Case study 7

A new child has arrived in your multi-cultural class. He is from Somalia. He has no English and he is reacting aggressively in the playground. Some of your pupils are chanting names behind his back and now several Afro-Caribbean boys are beginning to side with him.

What needs to be done quickly to preserve positive relationships between all these pupils?

What are you going to say to all the participants?

Remember, discuss these case studies with a colleague if you want further ideas. These examples in *Case study* 1 might help, but the only person in your situation, with your constraints, is you. The more you do yourself, with the help of colleagues, where necessary, the better.

◆ ACTIVITY 3.6 ◆◆◆

Let's use this Activity to look back at this Unit (and *Units 1* and *2* if necessary) and think about what you have written.

Read each question in the *Action plan* and respond in the spaces.

Action Plan

What pupil behaviour cannot be tolerated if I am going to establish a positive classroom atmosphere?

What teacher behaviour must not be tolerated if I am going to develop the right atmosphere in my classroom?

UNIT 4

How to Be an Assertive Teacher

◆ ACTIVITY 4.1 ◆◆◆

You will probably be the first to admit that the biggest problems you have in your classroom are to do with pupils who challenge your authority in such a way as to cause disruption and confrontation. Incidents like this will sap your energy, create rifts between you and your pupils and develop a tense and negative atmosphere.

Many of the problems you have will relate to pupil behaviour which is inappropriate. It is your reaction to your pupils' attitudes, actions and disruptions which will be a major factor in establishing good relationships.

Your behaviour, that is the way you relate to your pupils, *must* be ASSERTIVE and neither PASSIVE nor AGGRESSIVE.

Do you know the difference?

Alongside each of the following words write AS if you think behaving in this way is ASSERTIVE; AG if you feel it is AGGRESSIVE or PA if you think it shows PASSIVITY.

Angry		Volatile		Put upon		In control	
Confident		Lacking confidence		Hot tempered		Dominant	
Timid		Firm		Fair		Violent	
Quiet		Mild		Thoughtful		Meek	
Out of control		Complaisant		Knowledgeable			

◆ ACTIVITY 4.2 ◆◆◆

You should have placed AS for ASSERTION alongside the following words.

Read each one and use the space to say why you think behaving in this way will improve your teaching style, classroom management skills and your general all-round ability.

Confident:
Knowledgeable:
Firm:
Fair:
In control:
Thoughtful:

An interesting decision has to be taken about the word *Quiet*. Where would you put it?

◆ ACTIVITY 4.3 ◆◆◆

If it is possible to suggest why it is better for your teaching, your pupils' learning and the relationships in your classroom for you to be ASSERTIVE, it should be relatively easy to say why being AGGRESSIVE is inappropriate and counter-productive.

The following words from *Activity 4.1* suggest AGGRESSIVE behaviour. In each space say why behaving in this way would not help you be a better teacher.

Angry:
Dominant:
Volatile:
Hot tempered:
Out of control:
Violent:

◆ ACTIVITY 4.4 ◆◆◆

If being angry doesn't help you in your relationships with your pupils, neither does PASSIVITY. Why not?

Read each PASSIVE word and suggest why this behaviour will not help you in your classroom.

Timid:
Meek:
Put upon:
Lacking confidence:
Mild:
Complaisant:

◆ ▓ ACTIVITY 4.5 ▓ ◆◆◆

Before tackling some case studies, let's look at ways of defining the three terms we have been using.

✤ *Aggressiveness*: This means trying to get your own way by making other people feel useless, worthless or small. It doesn't always have to involve conflict, but it usually does either by causing verbal or even physical hostility.

✤ *Assertiveness*: This is all about being responsible for your own behaviour by respecting others and being honest. An assertive person is able to say what they want and feel but not at the expense of other people. It is also about being self-confident and positive and having the ability to handle conflict by reaching acceptable compromises.

✤ *Passivity*: This mean ignoring your own interests and allowing others to manipulate you. It often means denying your own feelings by not being active and pro-active and not recognising that you have needs and goals.

Read each *Case study* and respond in the space beneath each one.

Case study 1

You have had to speak firmly to a pupil for calling other members of the class names. He suddenly starts shouting at you and saying he hates you.

How would you respond passively to this situation?

How would you respond aggressively to this situation?

How would you respond assertively?

Case study 2

You are convinced that one of your pupils has stolen some money out of your desk. No one in the class has owned up and they have all denied having anything to do with it.

How would you react passively to this situation?

How would you react aggressively to this situation?

How would you react assertively?

Case study 3

For this particular lesson, you have arranged your class into groups. One of the groups has, after 30 minutes, done very little work. Another group starts whistling and a third is making paper aeroplanes.

How would you react aggressively to this situation?
How would you react passively?
How would you react assertively?

♦   **ACTIVITY 4.6**   ♦♦♦

If good relationships are to exist in your school and in your classroom, everyone, i.e. teachers, pupils and all other staff, must have rights.

Here are some of those rights. Before you go any further do remember that, by deciding to be an assertive teacher, you do not have to be assertive all the time and on all occasions.

Read each of these rights. It is important to think of them as applying to you, the teacher, and the pupil. In the spaces, suggest why you think this will help you improve your teaching and the kinds of relationships that can develop in your classroom.

I have the right to be heard and taken seriously.

Teachers have the right to set class priorities and pupils should have the opportunity to prioritise their own work.

I have the right to express feelings and opinions.

I have the right to say 'no'.

I have the right to make mistakes at times when I am trying my best.

I have the right to be in control of my own classroom space.

◆ ACTIVITY 4.7 ◆◆◆

When you are dealing with problems caused by pupils, it is possible to learn how to be assertive. This can also apply when you are dealing with colleagues and/or parents.

By being assertive in difficult circumstances, it is possible to improve your feelings about yourself, give yourself confidence and prevent yourself from feeling powerless and out of control.

This Activity gives you a step-by-step outline of what to do when you need to be assertive.

To create the script, let's go back to *Case study 1* in *Activity 4.5*.

> You have had to speak firmly to a pupil for calling other members of the class names. He suddenly starts shouting at you and saying he hates you.

All you have to do for this Activity is read the script in the *Step-by-step guide to assertion* below. It is quite long and you may feel that it is possible to shorten it. If you do, it is important not to lessen the meaning and the impact.

Step-by-step Guide to Assertion

> 1. SUMMARISE the behaviour that created the problem simply, unemotionally and straightforwardly.
>
> e.g. I do not like it when you call other people names and I certainly will not allow anyone to shout at me.
>
> 2. STATE exactly how *you* feel, not how anyone else feels.
>
> e.g. I am very concerned that you have been name calling and I am sad, upset and angry that you should feel that you have to shout at me in that bad tempered way.
>
> 3. DESCRIBE clearly and simply why you feel like this.
>
> e.g. First of all you know that you are expected to be friendly with everyone and I feel concerned because teasing and name calling is not being friendly. Shouting at a teacher makes me feel extremely unhappy because you know as well as anyone else that this is a very serious breach of the classroom and school rules.

4. SYMPATHISE OR EMPATHISE with the other person's point of view.

e.g. I can understand that you find some of your classmates irritating and I am sure I make you cross sometimes.

5. SPECIFY exactly what you would like the other person to do. You must also say what you would be willing to do to find a solution, a compromise or a way out of the situation in which you find yourself.

e.g. I want you to stop shouting instantly and I want you to promise me that you will stop calling other people names. If you have got a problem with some of your friends, you must tell me and I will try and help you.

6. DECIDE what your response will be. It is important that whatever you decide should clarify your position and not threaten the other person.

e.g. If you calm down immediately you will be able to stay in the classroom doing the same work as everyone else and I will talk to you later when you are less bad tempered.

There are other versions of assertive scripts in V. Rowland and K. Birkett, *Personal Effectiveness for Teachers* (Simon and Schuster, 1992).

◆ **ACTIVITY 4.8** ◆◆◆

It is important to write your own assertive script. If you don't try the techniques out using your own words, it will not become part of your own bank of strategies.

Here are three incidents where pupils have behaved badly. You have to deal with the problem and a useful way of doing this is to be ASSERTIVE.

Read each one and then use the following *Step-by-step guide to assertion* to write your own script.

Incident A

A colleague has been taking your class for ten minutes because you had been called away unexpectedly. When you return to the classroom, she tells you that one of the boys has sworn at her.

Incident B

There has been a fight in the playground and two girls from your class are brought into school by a lunchtime supervisor. They are both extremely red in the face and are scowling at you and at each other.

Incident C

There have been repeated messages that chewing gum is not allowed in school. One boy in your class or registration group is caught chewing for the third time this week.

Step-by-step Guide to Assertion

1. *Summarise A*:

    Summarise B:

    Summarise C:

---

2. *State A*:

    State B:

    State C:

---

3. *Describe A*:

    Describe B:

    Describe C:

---

4. *Sympathise/empathise A*:

    Sympathise/empathise B:

    Sympathise/empathise C:

---

5. *Specify A*:

    Specify B:

    Specify C:

---

6. *Decide A*:

    Decide B:

    Decide C:

◆ ACTIVITY 4.9 ◆◆◆

If you are going to be assertive, you have to match what you say to how you say it. In other words, you have to use appropriate body language.

Here are some descriptions of body language which should have an impact on your pupils.

Read each one and use the space to describe a situation either when you have used this kind of body language or when you might decide to use it in future.

Assertive body posture

Walking into a room upright, tall and dignified
Standing straight, head held high, balanced on both feet
If you are sitting when someone comes to talk to you about a difficult problem, you immediately stand up

Voice

A firm, clear and steady voice
A warm, sincere voice
Fluent, unhesitating speech which emphasises key words

Facial expressions and eye contact

Maintaining eye contact without staring
Open, friendly smile that isn't tight-lipped or fixed
Firm expression without smiling

◆ ACTIVITY 4.10 ◆◆◆

Let's end this Unit by examining one more technique in assertiveness which can be used in most situations.

It is called REPETITION and, as the name suggests, is a strategy where you keep repeating the same message that you are trying to get across.

This technique is particularly useful in situations where there is conflict and where you are telling someone something, correcting him/her or expressing an opinion that the pupil is trying either to deny, or not to hear.

This strategy usually works because pupils find it uncomfortable to listen to the repetition for too long.

Many challenging pupils are masters of the art of sidetracking and introducing irrelevant information. Keep calm and, using the appropriate body language, keep repeating the point you are wanting to make.

Read this REPETITION. You (T) are telling a pupil (P) not to run in the corridor. The pupil is agitated and denying it, although you saw it happen.

T: I don't want to see you running in the corridor again.
P: It wasn't me. I was walking.
T: You were not walking, you were running and I do not want to see you doing it again.
P: There were lots of other people doing it.
T: That is not the point. The point is that you were running in the corridor and you must not do it again.
P: I was in a hurry to get to Mrs Smith's lesson.
T: Let me say it again: I don't ever want to see you running in the corridor again.
. . .

What body language would you feel was appropriate?

◆ ACTIVITY 4.11 ◆◆◆

Use the following incident and write an imaginary repetitive script. Remember, you are being persistent and you are not losing your temper.

A pupil has gone out of school at lunchtime to the chip shop. He has been caught by a lunchtime supervisor and is arguing.

What body language will be appropriate?

◆ ACTIVITY 5.1 ◆◆◆

As a teacher in a classroom, you are the first strand in a web of complex relationships which will exist throughout the school. In the interests of your pupils' all-round development and in order to develop high quality teaching and learning experiences, you will have to work hard at the classroom level to create and nurture the most appropriate teacher-pupil relationships.

Managing pupils in the classroom in the best way possible will help you achieve positive relationships. In other words, you will have to have effective teaching and group management skills.

Read each of the skills and tick the most appropriate box. Underneath each one, write down what effect using this skill well would have on pupil-teacher relationships. Consider your own performance and, if you feel you are not good at the skill, describe the effect this has.

Effective Teaching Skills

As an effective teacher who wants to develop positive relationships I can . . .	Poor	Average	Good
1. . . . act as a guide and mentor to pupils			
2. . . . modify language and behaviour to meet pupils' needs			

3. . . . mark pupils' work so they can learn positively from any mistakes			
4. . . . differentiate and be responsive to different pupils' attitudes and needs			
5. . . . take account of any adverse factors outside the school that might affect pupils			
6. . . . incorporate obvious pupil interests into individual lessons and future plans			
7. . . . successfully collect information in order to assess individual pupils			

8. . . . recognise and take into account any reasons why pupils fail, and, if necessary, make changes			
9. . . . recognise which resources will be the most useful in satisfying pupils' needs			

◆ **ACTIVITY 5.2** ◆◆◆

Most pupils will work hard and have a positive relationship with teachers who are FIRM, FAIR and CONSISTENT.

Methods of control within the classroom have to be aimed at minimising disruption, because disruptive pupils negate any kind of relationship you are establishing and prevent you teaching and your pupils learning.

This Activity requires you to observe your own behaviour within the classroom during a period of a few days.

Over a period of a week, note down every single disruptive incident which stopped you teaching, stopped other pupils learning and made you have to do something to prevent the incident happening again. Use the following *Observation of disruptive incidents* chart to write down each incident. This provides space for three incidents. You may want to copy the chart to provide space for others.

At the same time, write down what action you took and whether it worked.

In the final box, try to decide whether this kind of disruptive incident jeopardises and undermines the positive relationships which you have developed in your classroom.

A disruptive incident.

Observation of Disruptive Incidents

Incident:
Action taken:
Comment on your success:
How did the incident affect relationships?
Incident:
Action taken:
Comment on your success:
How did the incident affect relationships?
Incident:
Action taken:
Comment on your success:
How did the incident affect relationships?

◆ ACTIVITY 5.3 ◆◆◆

From *Activity 5.2*, you should be able to identify the actions you take that work best. It is worth making sure that you remember them, because one of the ways good teachers remain successful, is by learning from their achievements.

So far, this Unit has allowed you to look at various kinds of teacher behaviour that should not only create a classroom atmosphere where relationships can flourish, but should also prevent as much disruptive behaviour as possible.

Let's look more closely at teacher behaviour while working in the classroom. The best way of doing this Activity is to work with a trusted colleague. If this is not possible, you can do it on your own.

If you use a colleague, you will both have to read the instructions and descriptions carefully before s/he observes you teach.

If you are doing it on your own, you will have to observe yourself. This will mean honesty and truthful self-appraisal.

It identifies six aspects of a teacher's behaviour.

✤ *Teacher giving help to pupils*: This relates to how you work with pupils who either need help because they are finding the work difficult, or are off-task and, perhaps, misbehaving.

✤ *Spoken behaviour*: This is how you use your voice with pupils.

✤ *Non-verbal behaviour*: This is concerned with how you use your body as part of your teaching style.

✤ *Eye contact*: This is how you actually look at pupils and can apply to when you are praising them or admonishing them for any reason.

✤ *Reaction to disruption and conflict*: This relates to the time spent dealing with disruption.

✤ *Control style*: This includes some of the ways problems are dealt with.

To complete the Activity, whether you are observing yourself, or asking a colleague to observe you, you will need to choose a time. Ideally, it should be approximately 30 minutes and should be after you have started the lesson, not during the first 10–15 minutes.

Make sure that you are familiar with the *Teacher style* sheet and use it to take detailed notes of what happens in the lesson.

Do you have a confident stance?

Teacher Style

	Length of time	Comments
Teacher help whilst working with girl pupils		
with boy pupils		
Spoken behaviour Firm, decisive, confident voice		
Lacking in confidence, unclear and mumbling		
Loud, shouting		
Speaking too quickly		
Speaking monotonously		
Using too harsh a voice		
Non-verbal behaviour Confident stance		
Confident smile		
Assertive use of body		
Walking around the room		
Standing at front facing class		

Frowning		
Standing close to pupils during a disruptive incident		
Eye contact Darting here and there		
Clear and direct to the class		
Clear and direct to individuals		
Used with raised eyebrows		
Glaring at pupils		
Frowning at disruptive pupils		
Disruption and conflict Handling it so incidents stop		
Handling it so the incident continues		
Control style Trying to ignore disruption		
Moving towards disruptive pupil and staying until disruption is over		

Using direct eye contact and brief stare		
Giving a direct instruction		
Frowning and glaring using eye contact		
Using humour to defuse a disruptive incident		
Making an assertive statement		
Sending pupil out of room		
Reminding pupils of the class rules		
Displaying obvious anger over the disruption		

◆ **ACTIVITY 5.4** ◆◆◆

As a short Activity to serve as a reminder, read through your *Teacher style* sheet and discuss it with your colleague if you have worked that way. The aim is to write down successful styles and those that were obviously less effective. Save your notes for the final *Action plans*.

◆ **ACTIVITY 5.5** ◆◆◆

In the previous Activity, you may have recognised some of the styles from earlier Units. There is obviously a certain amount of overlap. What each Activity is doing is building up a picture which will help you recognise appropriate ways of working that will improve and develop pupil-teacher relationships.

Here are three different groups of styles. *Don't* read them through beforehand, just read each one and give it a rating on a five-point scale:

> 5 . . . If it is a technique you use frequently
> 3 . . . If you sometimes use it
> 1 . . . It it is a technique or style you hardly ever use

Remember, you are reading each one and taking decisions about the rating you give it based on you, as a teacher. Be honest and truthful.

Teacher Techniques/Styles

	Rating score
Group 1 Demands instant obedience	
Tells pupils what to do and rarely, if ever, allows any freedom of choice	
Uses a harsh, forbidding tone of voice most, if not all, of the time	
Threatens very frequently	
Hardly ever gives choices	
Uses stock phrases for almost every incident, e.g. 'What do you think you are doing?', 'How dare you do that?', 'Don't think you're going to get away with that'	
Nags repeatedly	
Often makes unrealistic demands by treating all pupils as the same	

Is hostile and aggressive when disruption occurs	
TOTAL	
Group 2 Communicates directly and assertively what is wanted	
Achieves obedience without lowering self-esteem	
Is respectful even when driven to anger	
Tries not to react to incidents as they arise but, if possible, has a planned strategy	
Demands eye contact from a close distance without encroaching on pupil's personal space	
Speaks clearly, firmly and politely	
Always tries to distinguish between the person and the disruptive incident	
Expects obedience	
After an incident, always gets back to the original working relationship	
TOTAL	
Group 3 Uses body language in a non-assertive way	
In dealing with a disruptive incident, often uses a prolonged dialogue with the pupil	
Often gives pupils the feeling that it is wrong to tell them what to do	
Doesn't use a forceful tone of voice	
Often gets angry and yells	

Feels guilty about getting angry and shouting	
Sees disruption as unusual and threatening, giving the feeling of failure	
Often allows pupils to decide on what teachers' expectations of good behaviour are	
Hopes that friendliness is enough to ensure good relationships	
TOTAL	

◆ ACTIVITY 5.6 ◆◆◆

Add up your scores for each group in *Activity 5.5*.

If you scored highest in *Group 1*, you are more likely to be an AUTHORITARIAN teacher.

If you scored highest in *Group 2*, you will probably be a DECISIVE teacher.

If *Group 3* was your highest score, you may be a rather INDECISIVE teacher.

If none of the groups were significantly higher than the others, it could be that you are a teacher who uses a mixture of styles.

Here are the definitions of the three styles:

Authoritarian teacher

Teachers who behave in this way see power over pupils as an end in itself and, in order to gain and sustain this power, use embarrassment and humiliation as a technique. In a sense, it is a defensive 'us' and 'them' situation where the teacher must win at all costs. This teacher dislikes the use of co-operative group work as a style of teaching. S/he can be hostile, rude and aggressive and, rather than reflect on the success of his/her own practice, always blames the

An authoritarian teacher.

Decisive teacher

Rather than just stating the rules, this teacher negotiates and develops them with the pupils. Within a few days of meeting a class, this kind of teacher will develop strategies for handling misbehaviour. S/he recognises the inevitability of certain kinds of minor disruption and adopts the necessary techniques. Co-operation is encouraged by not creating an 'us' and 'them' situation. This teacher is good at humour, repartee and general pupil-teacher conversation, likes the pupils and, rather than nag, is brief, calm and always assertive.

Indecisive teacher

This teacher nearly always knows what to do in the classroom but not necessarily how to do it. It is often a case of wanting to be liked and yet not knowing how to go about achieving this state. Whilst not wanting to show anger and bad temper, such teachers don't know how to assert their rights and allow pupils to dominate proceedings and create their own classroom rules. Rather than issue direct statements and commands, indecisive teachers often enter into fruitless dialogues with pupils who are disruptive and sometimes lose their temper violently with consequent guilt.

Use the spaces below to write down the kinds of relationships you would expect to find in classrooms dominated by each teaching style.

Authoritarian:
Decisive:
Indecisive:

♦ **ACTIVITY 5.7** ♦♦♦

Now is the time to think carefully about the responses you have made throughout this handbook.

You need to create short *Action plans* which should be a summary of your intentions for developing and improving the teacher-pupil and pupil-pupil relationships in your classroom. Read each question and respond in the appropriate spaces. Refer to it regularly to remind yourself of those intentions.

Action Plans

Throughout this handbook, there are lists of teaching skills. List at least *five* of these skills which you will use to improve classroom relationships.
1.
2.
3.
4.
5.

What rules will you adopt? List up to *five*.

1.

2.

3.

4.

5.

What sanctions and reward will you use?

Sanction	Reward
1.	
2.	
3.	
4.	
5.	

If you are going to be a DECISIVE and ASSERTIVE teacher, what will you actually do?

As a final reminder to yourself, what exactly are the relationships you want in your classroom?

Further Reading

Alexander, R., Rose, J. and Woodhead, C., *Curriculum Organisation and Classroom Practice in Primary Schools* (DES, 1992)

Bennett, N. *et al., The Quality of Pupils' Learning Experience* (LEA, London, 1984)

Elton *et al., Report of the Committee of Enquiry: Discipline in Schools* (HMSO, 1989)

HMI, *Education in England 1990–91: The Annual Report of HM Senior Inspector of Schools* (DES, 1992)

Montgomery, D., *Managing Behaviour Problems* (Hodder and Stoughton, London, 1989)

Mortimore, P. *et al., School Matters: The Junior Years* (Open Books, Wells, 1988)

Rogers, B., *You Know the Fair Rule* (Longman, London, 1991)

Rutter, M. *et al., Fifteen Thousand Hours: Secondary Schools and their Effect on Pupils* (Open Books, Wells, 1979)

Saunders, M., *Class Control and Behaviour Problems* (McGraw-Hill, New York, 1979)

Smith, R., 'What makes a good teacher', *Child Education* (December 1988)

Smith, R., 'Fail proof policy: raising children's self esteem', *Child Education* (May 1990)

Smith, R., *The Effective School, Volume 2: Classroom Techniques and Management* (Framework Press, Lancaster, 1990)

Smith, R., *Managing Pupil Behaviour in School and Classroom: In-house Training Materials for Teachers* (Framework Press, Lancaster, 1993)

Smith, R., *Managing Your Classroom: A Guide to Better Teaching* (Framework Press, Lancaster, 1994)

Solity, J. and Raybould, B., *A Teacher's Guide to Special Needs* (OUP, Oxford, 1988)

Wragg, E.C., *Classroom Teaching Skills* (Croom Helm, London, 1984)